PEACE NOW

ANDREA DOLFI

INDIPENDENTLY PUBLISHED

to all those who fought for peace

We must be ready to make heroic sacrifices in favor of peace more willingly than we do in favor of war. There is no duty that I consider more important or to which I hold more strongly.

ALBERT EINSTEIN

CONTENTS

INTRODUCTION

◆ ◆ ◆

Pacifism is a philosophy and a social movement that represents the rejection of war and the promotion of peace. The history of pacifism is rich and varied, with roots dating back to ancient religious and philosophical traditions, but it found a more structured identity starting in the 19th century. During the 19th century, pacifism developed as a current of ideas and a movement aimed at preventing and countering war. Before this period, the issue of peace and war was the prerogative of heads of state and monarchs. However, during the 19th century, private citizens began to associate themselves to influence peace policy. The first pacifist associations arose in the United States in 1815, promoted by Quakers, and later spread to Europe. In 1907, Italian Ernesto Teodoro Moneta received the Nobel Peace Prize, marking an important moment for Italian pacifism. In the 20th century, figures like Leo Tolstoy and Mahatma Gandhi revived interest in pacifism through their practices of nonviolent resistance. Gandhi, in particular, inspired many other pacifist and civil rights movements, such as Martin Luther King Jr.'s in the United States. Modern pacifism continues to be an active movement, intertwined with other causes such as civil rights, women's emancipation, human rights, self-determination of peoples, and environmental defense. Its goal remains to prevent wars and reduce violence among human beings. In the final chapter, a possible answer to the question: Why the current escalation of global conflicts?

CHAPTER ONE. PACIFISM IN ANCIENT TRADITIONS

◆ ◆ ◆

Pacifism in ancient religious traditions is a fascinating theme that reflects humanity's universal search for peace and harmony. Many ancient world religions and philosophies have promoted principles of non-violence and respect for life.

For example, Buddhism is known for its teaching to abstain from any act of violence against any living creature. The concept of ahiṃsā, which means non-violence, is also fundamental in other Indian religions such as Hinduism, Jainism and has profoundly influenced pacifist thought and practices. In ancient Rome, despite being a heavily militarized society, examples of pacifist aspirations can be found, especially during periods of civil wars that led many to desire peace. These sentiments have also been expressed in literature, such as in the works of poets such as Virgil and Horace, who longed for havens of peace and expressed a desire to escape the reality of war.

These pacifist principles have continued to influence human thought and actions through the centuries, leading to more structured and organized pacifist movements in the modern era. Nonviolence has become a powerful force for social change, as demonstrated by the historical figures who have adopted and promoted these principles to combat injustice and promote peace around the world. Buddhism and pacifism are closely intertwined, as the core principles of Buddhism emphasize non-violence and compassion towards all living beings. The doctrine of ahiṃsā (non-violence) is central to Buddhist teaching and is reflected in the way Buddhists approach life and conflicts.

These pacifist principles have continued to influence human thought and actions through the centuries, leading to more structured and organized pacifist movements in the modern era. Nonviolence has become a powerful force for social change, as demonstrated by the historical figures who have adopted and promoted these principles to combat injustice and promote peace around the world. Buddhism and pacifism are closely intertwined, as the core principles of Buddhism emphasize non-violence and compassion towards all living beings. The doctrine of ahiṃsā (non-violence) is central to Buddhist teaching and is reflected in the way Buddhists approach life and conflicts.

Buddhism encourages its followers to actively engage in creating a peaceful society, not only through meditation and spiritual practice, but also through concrete actions in the world. This commitment is manifested in educational initiatives, interreligious dialogues and social interventions that aim to reduce suffering and promote understanding and harmony among people.

The concept of ahiṃsā is one of the fundamental principles of Indian religions and represents non-violence and respect for all forms of life. The Sanskrit word ahiṃsā is composed of "a", which means "not", and "hiṃsā", which is a desirative form of the verb "han", which means "to kill" or "to harm". Thus, ahiṃsā literally translates to "non-violence" or "non-harmfulness". In Hinduism, ahiṃsā indicates a broader concept of the absence of violence, which includes not only refraining from killing or physically harming, but also the promotion of positive values such as compassion, friendship and kindness. This principle was emphasized in the ancient texts of the Upaniṣads as early as the ninth century BC, and the term appears for the first time in the Chāndogya Upaniṣad.

In Jainism, ahiṃsā is the most important precept and manifests itself in a rigorous practice that includes abstaining from eating meat and being careful not to cause harm to any living being, even unintentionally. In Buddhism, ahiṃsā is interpreted as an ethical and spiritual commitment to avoid causing suffering to others. This extends beyond mere physical non-violence and includes thoughts, words, and actions that are free from harmful intentions.

The concept of ahiṃsā was spread in the West mainly through the actions and teachings of Mahatma Gandhi, who used non-violence as a tool of political resistance and social change. Gandhi inspired many non-violent political movements around the world, demonstrating the effectiveness of ahiṃsā as a philosophy of life and as an approach to conflict resolution.

In summary, ahiṃsā is a principle that transcends religious and cultural barriers, offering a universal vision of peace and harmony that can be applied in various contexts of human life.

Virgilio and Orazio, two of the greatest poets of ancient Rome, often explored themes of peace and the ideal of a life away from war and conflict in their works. Here are some examples:

Virgilio:

- In the Bucolics, particularly in Eclogue I, Virgil creates a bucolic ideal, a peaceful refuge from the reality of the civil wars that plagued Rome.
- In Eclogue IV, there is the theme of the Golden Age, a mythical period of peace and prosperity that Virgil hoped could be brought back under the reign of Augustus.

Orazio:

- In Epodo 16, also known as the epode of the "fortunate islands", Horace imagines an idyllic place, far from the corruption and violence of Rome, where virtuous citizens can live in peace.

- In the Odes, Horace often celebrates the peace re-established by Augustus after years of civil conflict, as in Ode 4.15, where peace is seen as a precious gift and a return to order.

These works reflect the common desire to escape the reality of war and find refuge in an ideal world of peace and tranquility. Virgil and Horace use poetry to create visions of better worlds, expressing their hope for a more peaceful future.

The Eclogue I of Virgilio's Bucolics is a classic example of poetry that celebrates peace and country life as a refuge from the instability and violence of civil wars. Here are some significant steps:

Tityre, tu patulae recubans sub tegmine fagi

silvestrem tenui musam meditaris avena;

nos patriae finis et dulcia linquimus arva.

Nos patriam fugimus; tu, Tityre, lentus in umbra

formosam resonare doces Amaryllida silvas.

In these verses, Melibeus speaks to Tityrus, who is lying quietly in the shade of a large beech tree, playing the flute and teaching the forests to resound the name of Amaryllis, while he himself must leave his homeland.

O Meliboee, deus nobis haec otia fecit.

Namque erit ille mihi semper deus; illius aram

saepe tener nostris ab ovilibus imbuet agnus.

Tityrus responds to Melibeus, attributing his tranquility and security to the protection of a god, who granted him peace and freedom to remain in his lands. These verses reflect Virgil's desire for a simple and peaceful life, far from the conflicts and worries of the outside world. Nature is seen as a sanctuary, a place where you can find peace and contentment. In the Eclogue IV of the Bucolics, Virgil expresses his vision of a return to the golden age, a mythical period of peace and prosperity. Here is a famous passage that reflects this theme:

Ultima Cumaei venit iam carminis aetas;

magnus ab integro saeclorum nascitur ordo.

Iam redit et Virgo, redeunt Saturnia regna,

iam nova progenies caelo demittitur alto.

In these verses, Virgil speaks of the return of the golden age as predicted by the Cumaean Sibyl, with the advent of a new great cycle of centuries. The Virgin (Virgo) and the realms of Saturn (Saturnia reign) are symbols of an era of justice and peace that was hoped to be inaugurated under the reign of Augustus. This passage is often interpreted as a prophecy of the birth of a divine child (puer) who would bring with him an era of peace and prosperity, symbolizing Virgil's hopes for a bright future under the leadership of Augustus. Virgil uses a language rich in imagery and symbolism to evoke the hope of a renewed world, free from the suffering and wars of the past, a world in which humanity can live in harmony with nature and the gods.

In these verses, Virgil speaks of the return of the golden age as predicted by the Cumaean Sibyl, with the advent of a new great cycle of centuries. The Virgin (Virgo) and the realms of Saturn (Saturnia reign) are symbols of an era of justice and peace that was hoped to be inaugurated under the reign of Augustus. This passage is often interpreted as a prophecy of the birth of a divine child (puer) who would bring with him an era of peace and prosperity, symbolizing Virgilio's hopes for a bright future under the leadership of Augustus. Virgilio uses a language rich in imagery and symbolism to evoke the hope of a renewed world, free from the suffering and wars of the past, a world in which humanity can live in harmony with nature and the gods.

nos manet Oceanus circum vagus: arva beata

petamus, arva divites et insulas,

reddit ubi cererem tellus inarata quotannis

et inputata floret usque vinea,

germinat et numquam fallentis termes olivae

suamque pulla ficus ornat arborem,

mella cava manant ex ilice, montibus altis

levis crepante lympha desilit pede.

In these verses, Orazio expresses the desire to escape to the fortunate islands, where the land produces abundantly without the need for ploughing, the vines bloom without being pruned, the olive and fig trees bear fruit generously, and honey flows from the oaks. It is an image of abundance and peace, a stark contrast to the reality of war and conflict.

This passage reflects Orazio's desire to find refuge in an ideal world, a dream of peace that opposes the turbulence and corruption of urban life in Rome.

In Ode 4.15, Orazio celebrates the peace re-established by Augustus after years of civil conflict, extolling peace as a precious gift and a return to order. Here is a significant passage that reflects this theme:

Phoebus volentem proelia me loqui

victas et urbes increpuit lyra,

ne parva Tyrrhenum per aequor

vela darem. Tua, Caesar, aetas

fruges et agris rettulit uberes

et signa nostro restituit Iovi

derepta Parthorum superbis

postibus et vacuum duellis

Ianum Quirini clausit et ordinem

rectum evaganti frena licentiae

iniecit, emovitque culpas

et veteres revocavit artes,

per quas Latinum nomen et Italae

crevere vires famaque et imperi

porrecta maiestas ad ortus

solis ab Hesperio cubili.

In these verses, Orazio describes how Apollo dissuaded him from singing about battles and conquered cities, prompting him instead to celebrate the age of Augustus. The age of Augustus brought abundant fruit to the fields, returned the Roman insignia stolen by the Parthians, closed the temple of Janus, a symbol of the end of wars, and restored order and discipline, renewing the ancient virtues that made Rome great.

This passage is a praise of the Augustan age, seen as an era of peace and prosperity, a return to the order and morality that had characterized the best times of Rome. Pacifism, understood as the search for peace and the rejection of violence, finds significant expression in both the Old and New Testaments, although not always in explicit or systematic terms.

In the Old Testament, the concept of peace is often

linked to God's promise of a future of prosperity and harmony for his people. An example is the famous passage from Isaiah (2:4) that speaks of the transformation of the instruments of war into agricultural instruments: "He will judge among the nations, and will be the arbiter of many peoples; they shall beat their swords into plowshares, and their spears into pruning hooks; nation against nation will no longer lift up the sword, they will no longer train themselves in the art of war." This passage reflects the vision of a world in which violence is overcome and peace reigns supreme.

In the New Testament, Jesus Christ is often seen as a pacifist figure, especially in his teaching on love of enemies and non-resistance to evil with evil. In the Gospel of Matthew (5:9), Jesus says, "Blessed are the peacemakers, for they shall be called children of God." In addition, the Gospel of Luke (6:27-31) records Jesus' words encouraging us to love our enemies and do good to those who hate us.

Pacifism is a theme present in the Qur'an and in the Islamic tradition. A Qur'anic verse states that God does not approve of war and does not love those who sow disorder on the earth. The life of the Prophet Muhammad shows that war was seen as a means of defense in inevitable situations. During the early years of the Qur'anic revelation, Muslims suffered persecution without resorting to violence, promoting peace instead. Only after a specific revelation, granting permission to fight to those who had been attacked, did the Prophet command to prepare for war, but only for defensive purposes.

In addition, the Qur'an warns against provocation and the use of unnecessary violence. The term "holy war" does not exist in the original lexicon of Islam; The word "gihad" means "effort" and refers primarily to an act of spiritual and defensive resistance.

In conclusion, the Islamic principles proclaimed in the Qur'an explain a peaceful and moderate policy, as demonstrated by the life of the Prophet Muhammad and his actions, which included the signing of peace agreements and the bloodless conquest of Mecca. A fundamental principle of Judaism is the concept of "shalom" (peace), which is one of the highest values. The search for peace is seen as a moral and spiritual obligation. The Talmud, for example, teaches that "the Torah was given to promote peace in the world" (Gittin 59b), and many Jewish prayers and blessings include calls for peace.

CHAPTER TWO. PEACE IN CATHOLICISM AFTER THE REFORM OF THE SECOND VATICAN COUNCIL

◆ ◆ ◆

The Second Vatican Council, which took place between the 1962 liturgical reform, in particular, introduced the use of vernacular languages in celebrations, allowing the faithful to participate more actively and better understand the rites.

In terms of peace, the Council promoted a more open and dialoguing approach to other religions and cultures, emphasizing the importance of mutual understanding and respect. This change in attitude has helped to create a more conducive environment for peace, both within the Church and in her relations with the outside world.

Peace, as a concept, has therefore been reinterpreted not only as the absence of conflict, but as an active commitment to justice, solidarity and the common good, thus reflecting a more inclusive and global vision of the role of the Church in the modern world.

Since the Second Vatican Council, ecumenism has become a fundamental aspect in the search for peace in the Catholic world. The decree Unitatis Redintegratio emphasized the importance of re-establishing unity among all Christians as one of the main objectives of the Council. This document encouraged dialogue and understanding between the different Christian confessions, recognizing that almost all, albeit in different ways, aspire to a unique and visible Church of God.

The ecumenical movement, which had developed at the beginning of the twentieth century, was welcomed and strengthened by the Council, which saw in the action of the Holy Spirit the driving force behind this search for unity. Ecumenical dialogue was therefore understood not only as a way to overcome historical divisions, but also as a tool to promote peace in the world, through collaboration and mutual knowledge between the different Christian traditions.

The ecumenical movement, which had developed at the beginning of the twentieth century, was welcomed and strengthened by the Council, which saw in the action of the Holy Spirit the driving force behind this search for unity. Ecumenical dialogue was therefore understood not only as a way to overcome historical divisions, but also as a tool to promote peace in the world, through collaboration and mutual knowledge between the different Christian traditions.

The decree Unitatis Redintegratio was one of the most important documents of the Second Vatican Council in terms of ecumenism and peace. Published on November 21, 1964, it marked a significant change in the attitude of the Catholic Church towards other Christian denominations.

The document recognizes that division among

Christians is contrary to the will of Christ and harmful to the world, hindering the preaching of the Gospel. Therefore, it promotes a renewed commitment to Christian unity, emphasizing that all, despite differences, aspire to a unique and visible Church of God.

Unitatis Redintegratio invites the Catholic faithful to an attitude of fraternal respect and knowledge of other Christian confessions, promoting ecumenical dialogue as a means of achieving unity. This dialogue is seen not only as a way to overcome historical divisions, but also as an essential tool for promoting peace in the world.

Peace, therefore, is understood as the fruit of unity and harmony among Christians, which can have a positive impact on society as a whole. Ecumenism, according to the Council, is a path that all Christians are called to travel together, with the aim of building bridges of understanding and collaboration, for the common good and for the glory of God.

Pope Francis' apostolic encyclicals have addressed the theme of peace in depth, emphasizing the importance of fraternity and dialogue as foundations for lasting peace. Among the most significant in this context, we can mention:

- *Fratelli tutti* (October 3, 2020): In this encyclical on fraternity and social friendship, Pope Francis explores the concept of peace as a path that requires commitment and action. It emphasizes that real and lasting peace is only possible through a global ethic of solidarity and cooperation, serving a future shaped by interdependence and co-responsibility in the entire human family.

- *Laudato si'* (May 24, 2015): Although primarily focused on the environment, this encyclical touches on the theme of peace, linking it to care for our common home. Pope Francis calls for an ecological conversion that includes respect for creation, justice for the poor and commitment to society, thus contributing to peace.

- *Lumen Fidei* (June 29, 2013): This first encyclical of Pope Francis' pontificate, completed by Benedict XVI, speaks of the light of faith that guides humanity's journey towards peace and communion.

In these encyclicals, Pope Francis emphasizes that peace is not just the absence of war, but an active commitment to justice, truth, and mercy. Peace is seen as patient work that honors the memory of the victims and opens up to a common hope stronger than revenge. The encyclical "Fratelli tutti" in particular, describes peace as an artisanal work that involves everyone and that is achieved through concrete paths and transformations made by peoples.

The Second Vatican Council laid the foundations for a renewed commitment of the Catholic Church to the promotion of peace, emphasizing dialogue and reconciliation. Peace has been defined as "the fruit of the order brought into human society by its Founder and which must be brought about by men who thirst for ever more perfect justice" (Gaudium et Spes, 78).

Papal encyclicals continued to build on this foundation, with Pope John XXIII publishing "Pacem in Terris" in 1963, emphasizing peace founded on truth, justice, love, and freedom. Pope Francis, with his encyclical "Fratelli tutti", has further explored the concept of peace as a path of solidarity and cooperation.

As for the Ukrainian-Russian conflict, the most recent news indicates that the situation remains tense and complex. Despite attempts at mediation and calls for an end to the conflict, there are still no signs of a final peaceful resolution. The Church, following the teachings of the Second Vatican Council and subsequent encyclicals, could play a role in promoting dialogue and reconciliation in conflict situations such as this, in line with her mission of peace.

The role of the Ecumenical Church in the conflict in Palestine has been to promote peace and justice, seeking to be a bridge between different communities and to offer a moral and spiritual voice in a complex and painful situation. The Church has tried to play a role of mediation and encouragement of dialogue between the parties in conflict.

The World Council of Churches (WCC), for example, has condemned attacks on places of worship and called on the international community to strengthen the protection of shrines in Gaza. The Holy See expressed its full commitment to promoting peace and justice in Israel and Palestine, stressing the need to end violence and respect human rights.The Ecumenical Church, through various initiatives and statements, has sought to bring attention to the suffering of those affected by the conflict and to advocate for peaceful solutions that respect the dignity and rights of all individuals involved. The role of the Church in situations like this is crucial not only to offer humanitarian assistance and spiritual support, but also to work towards lasting reconciliation that can lead to a just and permanent peace.

CHAPTER THREE. PACIFISM IN THE NINETEENTH CENTURY

◆ ◆ ◆

Pacifism in the nineteenth century saw the birth of movements and ideas aimed at preventing and countering war. Before this period, the issue of peace was mainly handled by heads of state and monarchs. However, in the nineteenth century, private citizens began to associate to promote peace.

One of the most significant contributions came from the Quakers, who founded the first pacifist associations in the United States in 1815. These associations also spread rapidly in Europe, with the birth of the Society for the Promotion of Permanent and Universal Peace in England in 1816.

In continental Europe, the first pacifist association was the Peace Society, founded in 1830. This organization had not only religious but also political and economic motivations in its opposition to the war. Important pacifist congresses were held in London, Brussels, Paris and Frankfurt, with the Congress of the Friends of Peace in Paris considered the first international congress of pacifism.

In addition, the figure of women played a significant

role in the peace movement of the nineteenth century. Women engaged in pacifism often clashed with the misogynism of the time, but their contribution was fundamental to the spread of pacifist ideas and women's emancipation.

The first pacifist associations in the United States were born in 1815, mainly thanks to the initiative of the Quakers. The New York Peace Society was founded by David Dodge, a Quaker who promoted peace and the rejection of war. This society was one of the first organizations to seek to resolve international conflicts through arbitration rather than war.

David Low Dodge (1774-1852) was a prominent American activist and theologian, known for his pacifist efforts. Born in Brooklyn, Connecticut, Dodge was one of the founders of the New York Peace Society in 1815, one of the first peace organizations in the United States.

Dodge wrote some of the earliest anti-war pamphlets in America, including "The Mediator's Kingdom not of this World" (1809) and "War Inconsistent with the Religion of Jesus Christ" (1812). These writings expressed his belief that war was incompatible with the teachings of Jesus Christ and promoted arbitration as a method of resolving international conflicts.

The New York Peace Society was the first peace society founded in the United States, in 1815, by David Low Dodge. This organization has had several periods over the years:

1. First period (1815-1828): Founded immediately after the end of the War of 1812, the society organized weekly meetings and produced pacifist literature that was also

distributed abroad.

2. Second Period (1837-1844): Reformed in 1837, the society sought to prevent war against Mexico through negotiation, but dissolved in 1844.

3. Third period (1906-1940): Refounded in 1906, the society was active during World War I, organizing conferences and opposing American intervention.

In 1830, one of the first continental pacifist associations, the Society of Peace, was born in Europe. Founded by Jean-Jacques de Sellon in Geneva, this organization relied on religious, political, and economic motivations to oppose the war. The Geneva Peace Society promoted arbitration as a method of resolving international conflicts and organized congresses to discuss issues such as disarmament and cooperation between nations.

Jean-Jacques de Sellon (1782-1839) was a Swiss philanthropist, art collector, patron and pacifist. Born in Geneva, he is known for having founded the Peace Society, the first pacifist organization on the European continent, in 1830. De Sellon was a fervent supporter of universal peace and an active opponent of the death penalty.

In addition to his pacifist commitment, de Sellon was also a patron of the arts and a collector. It has hosted numerous illustrious personalities of its time, including members of the Bonaparte family, the pianist Franz Liszt and the statesman Camillo Benso, Count of Cavour.

CHAPTER FOUR. PACIFISM IN ITALY FROM ITS ORIGINS TO THE CONTEMPORARY PERIOD

◆ ◆ ◆

Pacifism in Italy has a long and complex history that spans various historical periods and social movements: The first pacifist ideas in Italy date back to the eighteenth century, when people began to talk about a real pacifist ideology. During this time, pacifism was often linked to religious and philosophical movements that promoted peace and tolerance.

In the nineteenth century, Italian pacifism developed further with the birth of various associations and movements. Among these, the Society of Peacefounded in Geneva by Jean-Jacques de Sellon in 1830, which also influenced Italian pacifist thought. During this period, pacifism was often linked to socialist and anarchist movements that saw war as an obstacle to social justice and freedom.

After the Second World War, pacifism in Italy was further strengthened. The devastation caused by the war led to a greater awareness of the need to promote peace. In the 1960s, the philosopher and educator Aldo Capitini organized the first March for Peace and

Brotherhood among Peoples from Perugia to Assisi in 1961, a symbolic event that brought together various strands of Italian pacifism: social-communist, Catholic and liberal-radical.

In recent decades, pacifism in Italy has continued to evolve, facing new challenges such as the wars in Kosovo and Iraq. Italian peace movements have coordinated in national and transnational networks, promoting non-violence and opposing military intervention. Recently, Italian pacifism has also gained visibility in relation to the Russian invasion of Ukraine, with movements advocating multilateral diplomacy and "active neutrality".

Before the First World War, pacifism in Italy was influenced by various social and political movements. During the nineteenth century, pacifism was often linked to socialist, anarchist and liberal movements that saw war as an obstacle to social justice and freedom. Some highlights of Italian pacifism before the First World War:

1. Socialist and Anarchist Movements: These movements were strongly opposed to war, seeing it as a tool of the ruling classes to maintain control and suppress popular uprisings.

2. Pacifist Associations: Several pacifist associations were born in this period, inspired by international movements such as the Peace Society founded in Geneva in 1830.

3. International Peace Congress: In 1907, Italy hosted the International Peace Congress in Milan, an event that brought together pacifists from around the world to discuss disarmament and peaceful conflict resolution.

4. Neutralism: At the outbreak of the First World War, Italy initially declared its neutrality. The majority of the population and many intellectuals and politicians were against entering the war.

Before the First World War, the Italian socialist and anarchist movements were strongly opposed to war, seeing it as a tool of the ruling classes to maintain control and suppress popular uprisings. The Italian socialists, influenced by pacifist and internationalist ideas, saw in the war a conflict between the ruling classes for the control of resources and power. The majority of Italian socialists were opposed to Italy's participation in the war, arguing that the conflict would only aggravate the living conditions of the working class.

Italian anarchists, such as those of the Milan Barrier, were the main protagonists of the Turin uprisings of 1917, opposing the war and promoting anti-militarism. During the First World War, the Milan Barrier was the scene of numerous protests against war and hunger. In 1917, an anti-war strike turned into a full-blown insurrection, with every corner of the neighborhood becoming a barricade. Local anarchists were protagonists of these struggles, opposing the war and promoting anti-militarism.

The International Peace Congress held in Milan in 1907 was a significant event in the global peace movement. This congress was organized by Ernesto Teodoro Moneta, an Italian journalist and patriot who received the Nobel Peace Prize in 1907 for his commitment to the promotion of peace and international arbitration.

Moneta, born in Milan in 1833, actively participated in the struggles of the Risorgimento before devoting himself to journalism and pacifism. He was director of the newspaper "Il Secolo" and founder of the Lombard Union for Peace and International Arbitration. His experiences in the wars of the Risorgimento led him to condemn violence and promote the peaceful resolution of conflicts.

The 1907 Milan International Peace Congress brought together pacifists from around the world to discuss issues such as disarmament, international arbitration, and cooperation among nations. This event represented an important platform for the peace movement, helping to spread ideas of peace and international cooperation.

During the Viet Nam War, a strong pacifist movement also developed in Italy that opposed the military intervention of the United States and supported the Vietnamese people. This movement was part of the broader context of the global protests of the 1960s and 1970s, which were characterized by strong opposition to war and violence. Numerous demonstrations were held in various Italian cities, involving students, intellectuals and workers. These protests were often organized by left-wing groups, trade unions, and student movements.

Il movimento pacifista italiano mostrò una forte solidarietà con il popolo vietnamita, organizzando raccolte di fondi e campagne di sensibilizzazione per sostenere la resistenza vietnamita contro l'aggressione americana.

La guerra del Vietnam e le proteste contro di essa influenzarono profondamente la cultura italiana dell'epoca, ispirando canzoni, film e opere letterarie che denunciavano la guerra e promuovevano la pace.

Il 15 ottobre 1969, l'Italia partecipò al Moratorium Day, una giornata di protesta globale contro la guerra del Vietnam. Questo evento vide la partecipazione di migliaia di persone in tutto il paese.The Italian peace movement showed strong solidarity with the Vietnamese people, organizing fundraisers and awareness campaigns to support the Vietnamese resistance against American aggression. The Viet Nam War and the protests against it profoundly influenced the Italian culture of the time, inspiring songs, films and literary works denouncing the war and promoting peace.

Numerous conferences and public debates were organized to discuss the implications of the war and promote peaceful solutions. In the 60s and 70s, several Italian intellectuals distinguished themselves for their pacifist commitment, opposing the Viet Nam War and promoting peace and social justice. Here are some of the most well-known:

1. Aldo Capitini (1899-1968) was a philosopher, pedagogue and pacifist activist. Founder of the Nonviolent Movement, Capitini organized the first March for peace and brotherhood among peoples from Perugia to Assisi in 1961. His ideas on nonviolence profoundly influenced the Italian peace movement.

2. Norberto Bobbio (1909-2004) was a philosopher, jurist and political scientist. Bobbio wrote numerous essays on peace and democracy, criticizing war and promoting dialogue and international cooperation.

3. Danilo Dolci (1924-1997) was a sociologist, poet and activist. Known as the "Italian Gandhi", Dolci promoted nonviolence and direct action to combat poverty and social injustice in Sicily.

4. Ernesto Balducci (1922-1992) was a priest and writer. Founder of the magazine "Testimonianze", Balducci was a fervent supporter of peace and human rights, opposing war and promoting dialogue between cultures.

5. Dario Fo (1926-2016) was a playwright, actor and director. Winner of the Nobel Prize for Literature in 1997, Fo used theatre as a tool for social and political criticism, opposing war and promoting peace through

his works.

These intellectuals, along with many others, helped form an Italian peace movement that opposed the Viet Nam War and promoted nonviolence and social justice. During the war in Kosovo, the Italian peace movement mobilized strongly against NATO military intervention. Italian military bases were used for air operations against Serbia, which sparked protests and demonstrations throughout the country. Italian pacifists organized marches, sit-ins and awareness campaigns to promote diplomatic solutions and denounce the humanitarian consequences of the conflict.

The opposition to the war in Iraq was one of the most significant moments for the Italian peace movement. On February 15, 2003, about three million people demonstrated in Rome against the imminent American attack on Iraq, in one of the largest pacifist protests in Italian history. The Italian peace movement joined international networks to call for an end to hostilities and promote peace through dialogue and diplomacy.

The Russian invasion of Ukraine has reactivated the Italian peace movement, which has organized numerous demonstrations and campaigns to demand an end to the conflict and promote diplomatic solutions. The Italian Peace and Disarmament Network, together with trade unions, associations and non-governmental organizations, led the mobilization, asking Europe not to take military sides but to relaunch mediation to stop the war. Italian pacifists argue that sending weapons is not an effective solution and promote "active neutrality" to protect those affected by the conflict.

The war in Kosovo and the fall of the Prodi government are closely linked events in the Italian political history of the 90s. The Kosovo War (1998–1999) was a conflict between Yugoslav forces and the Kosovo Liberation Army (KLA), culminating in NATO intervention in March 1999. Italy, as a member of NATO, participated in military operations, using its air bases for bombing missions.

Romano Prodi's first government fell on 9 October 1998, after being voted no in the Chamber of Deputies with 312 votes in favour and 313 against. The government crisis was caused by the withdrawal of external support from Rifondazione Comunista, which did not agree with the Italian military intervention in Kosovo.

The fall of the Prodi government came at a critical moment for international politics. A few days after the no-confidence vote, on October 12, 1998, NATO issued the Activation Order against Yugoslavia, preparing for military intervention.

CHAPTER FIVE.
AMERICAN PACIFISM

◆ ◆ ◆

Pacifism in the United States has deep roots and has manifested itself at various times in history through social movements, influential figures, and mass protests. This chapter explores the different stages of American pacifism, analyzing its origins, its evolutions, and its impact on society. The earliest expressions of pacifism in the United States date back to the colonial period, with religious groups such as the Quakers preaching nonviolence and peace. During the American Civil War, some individuals and groups opposed the war, promoting peaceful solutions to conflicts.

The Quakers, also known as the Society of Friends, have been among the most fervent advocates of pacifism in American history. During the American Civil War (1861-1865), their commitment to nonviolence and social justice manifested itself in various ways, despite hardship and persecution. The pacifism of the Quakers is based on the fundamental principles of their faith, which include the belief that each individual possesses an "inner light" of God and that violence is incompatible with the divine will. This belief led them to refuse any form of participation in the war, either as combatants or as supporters.

During the Civil War, the Quakers found themselves in a difficult position. While many North Americans saw war as a necessity to abolish slavery and preserve the Union, the Quakers remained true to their pacifist principles. They refused to join the army and, in many cases, paid fines or were imprisoned for their refusal.

Despite their opposition to the war, the Quakers did not remain inactive. Many of them engaged in humanitarian activities, providing medical assistance and support to the wounded and needy, regardless of their affiliation. This commitment to care and compassion reflected their values of equality and respect for human life.

The Quakers faced numerous challenges during the war. Their pacifist stance made them unpopular with many of their fellow citizens, and they were often accused of treason or lack of patriotism. Despite this, they remained firm in their principles, demonstrating remarkable moral courage. Quaker pacifism during the American Civil War is a significant example of how faith and moral principles can guide actions even in times of conflict. Their dedication to nonviolence and social justice has left a lasting imprint on American history, inspiring future generations of pacifists and peace activists.

With the entry of the United States into World War I, a strong peace movement emerged. Organizations such as the Women's Peace Party, founded by Jane Addams, and the American Union Against Militarism opposed military intervention and promoted diplomacy as a means of resolving international conflicts.

The peace movement faced numerous challenges during the war. With the entry of the United States into the conflict in 1917, the government took severe measures against dissidents. The Espionage Act of 1917 and the Sedition Act of 1918 were used to suppress pacifist voices, leading to the arrest and persecution of many activists.

Despite the difficulties, the peace movement managed to leave a lasting imprint. The ideas promoted during this period influenced future generations of peace activists and contributed to the formation of international organizations dedicated to the peaceful resolution of conflicts, such as the League of Nations.

The American peace movement during World War I represents an important chapter in the history of nonviolence and diplomacy. The challenges faced and achievements achieved by these activists continue to inspire those fighting for peace in the contemporary world.

During World War II, American pacifism faced significant challenges, as many citizens viewed war against Nazism as a moral necessity. However, after the war, the peace movement was reborn, especially during the Cold War, with protests against the nuclear arms race and aggressive military policies.

During World War II, the peace movement in the United States faced significant challenges. Although pacifism was an established school of thought, the entry of the United States into the war after the attack on Pearl

Harbor in 1941 made it difficult for pacifists to maintain a prominent position.

American pacifism during this period was supported by various religious and social groups. The Quakers, known for their long tradition of nonviolence, continued to promote peace and oppose war. Other organizations, such as the Fellowship of Reconciliation and the War Resisters League, also played an important role in keeping the peace voice alive.

Despite the difficulties, many American pacifists engaged in humanitarian activities. They provided medical assistance and support to the wounded and needy, both on the domestic and international fronts. This commitment reflected their values of compassion and respect for human life.

Among the key figures of American pacifism during World War II were Dorothy Day and the Catholic Workers' Movement, who opposed the war and promoted nonviolence and social justice. The Fellowship of Reconciliation, with leaders such as A.J. Muste, also continued to advocate for peace and oppose militarism.

American pacifism during World War II represents a complex and challenging chapter in the history of the peace movement. Despite hardship and persecution, pacifists remained true to their principles, demonstrating remarkable moral courage and helping to keep the tradition of nonviolence alive in the United States.

One of the most iconic periods for American pacifism was during the Viet Nam War. Millions of Americans, including students, intellectuals, and veterans, mobilized against the military intervention. Mass protests, marches and demonstrations became symbols of the peace movement. Figures such as Martin Luther King Jr. linked the struggle for civil rights with the cause of peace, promoting nonviolence as a tool for social change.

One of the most iconic periods for American pacifism was during the Viet Nam War. Millions of Americans, including students, intellectuals, and veterans, mobilized against the military intervention. Mass protests, marches and demonstrations became symbols of the peace movement. Figures such as Martin Luther King Jr. linked the struggle for civil rights with the cause of peace, promoting nonviolence as a tool for social change.

The Viet Nam War, fought between 1955 and 1975, was one of the most controversial conflicts of the twentieth century. During this period, the American peace movement emerged as a powerful force, influencing public opinion and policy decisions.

The anti-Viet Nam War peace movement had its roots in the United States, where the first protests were organized by university students and activist groups. Growing awareness of the atrocities of the war, combined with media coverage, fueled public outrage. The initial manifestations were often small and local, but over time they grew in scale and intensity.

Numerous prominent figures played a crucial role in the peace movement. John Lennon, with his song "Give Peace a Chance", has become a symbol of resistance against war. Martin Luther King Jr., known for his commitment to civil rights, has also spoken out against war, linking the struggle for social justice to the need for peace. Other activists such as Jane Fonda and Muhammad Ali have used their fame to publicly criticize the war and support the peace movement.

Protests against the Viet Nam War reached their peak in the 60s and 70s. One of the most significant demonstrations was the March on Washington in 1967, which was attended by hundreds of thousands of people. The protests were not limited to the United States; All over the world, people have come together to demand an end to the conflict. The demonstrations were often accompanied by acts of civil disobedience, such as refusing to join the army.

The peace movement has had a significant impact on American politics. Growing opposition to the war has led to a shift in public opinion, putting pressure on politicians to find a peaceful solution. In 1973, the Paris Agreement marked the beginning of the withdrawal of American troops from Viet Nam. Although the war continued until 1975, the peace movement has shown that collective action can influence political decisions and help end violent conflicts.

American pacifism during the Viet Nam War represented one of the largest mass mobilizations of the twentieth century. Through protests, demonstrations and acts of civil disobedience, millions of people have expressed their opposition to the war, influencing public opinion and political decisions. This movement has left a lasting legacy, demonstrating the power of non-violence and collective action.

Over the past few decades, pacifism in the United States has continued to evolve. Protests against the wars in Iraq and Afghanistan have seen a new generation of activists commit to peace. Organizations such as Veterans for Peace and Code Pink have played a crucial role in keeping the peace tradition alive.

American pacifism has undergone a remarkable evolution from the post-Viet Nam period to the present day. Here is an overview of the main milestones and transformations.

After the end of the Viet Nam War in 1975, the American peace movement continued to grow. The traumatic experiences of the conflict fueled a strong anti-war sentiment. During the 1980s, the movement focused primarily on the fight against nuclear weapons, culminating in large demonstrations such as the 1982 one in New York, which was attended by about a million people.

With the end of the Cold War, the peace movement had to adapt to a new geopolitical context. The campaigns focused on promoting global peace and preventing regional conflicts. During the 1991 Gulf War, there were numerous protests against the military intervention of the United States.

The attacks of September 11, 2001 and the subsequent wars in Afghanistan and Iraq have rekindled the peace movement. Millions of people around the world participated in demonstrations against the invasion of Iraq in 2003, one of the largest global protests in history.

In recent years, the peace movement has faced new challenges, including international terrorism, refugee crises, and geopolitical tensions. However, it continues to promote non-violence and the peaceful resolution of conflicts. Recent campaigns have also focused on issues such as climate change, recognizing the link between peace and environmental sustainability.

American pacifism has demonstrated remarkable adaptability and resilience, continuing to influence politics and society through decades of global change.

American pacifism has had a significant impact on the country's history, influencing public policy and promoting a culture of nonviolence and dialogue. Although it has faced many challenges, the peace movement continues to be an important voice in American society, reminding us of the importance of peace and diplomacy.

American pacifism in 2024 continues to be a significant force, even as it faces new challenges and global contexts. Here are some key aspects of the peace movement today.

The American peace movement is active in several campaigns, including those against ongoing wars and the proliferation of nuclear weapons. Events such as the Arena di Pace 2024 were attended by thousands of people, emphasizing the importance of disarmament and nonviolence.

In addition to traditional anti-war campaigns, pacifism today is intertwined with other global issues such as climate change and human rights. Many pacifists see the fight for climate justice as an integral part of promoting peace, recognizing that conflicts often arise from scarce resources and inequalities.

The peace movement faces criticism and challenges, especially in the current complex geopolitical context. The wars in Ukraine and the Middle East have raised debates about how to balance pacifism with the need to defend human rights and national sovereignty.

The new generations of activists are bringing new energy and perspectives to the peace movement. They use social media to organize and spread messages of peace, reaching a global and diverse audience.

American pacifism, therefore, continues to evolve, adapting to the changes of the modern world and seeking to promote a culture of peace and nonviolence. The American peace movement is active in several campaigns, including those against ongoing wars and the proliferation of nuclear weapons. Events such as the Arena di Pace 2024 were attended by thousands of people, emphasizing the importance of disarmament and nonviolence.

In addition to traditional anti-war campaigns, pacifism today is intertwined with other global issues such as climate change and human rights. Many pacifists see the fight for climate justice as an integral part of promoting peace, recognizing that conflicts often arise from scarce resources and inequalities.

The peace movement faces criticism and challenges, especially in the current complex geopolitical context. The wars in Ukraine and the Middle East have raised debates about how to balance pacifism with the need to defend human rights and national sovereignty.

The new generations of activists are bringing new energy and perspectives to the peace movement. They use social media to organize and spread messages of peace, reaching a global and diverse audience.

American pacifism, therefore, continues to evolve, adapting to the changes of the modern world and seeking to promote a culture of peace and nonviolence.

CHAPTER SIX. THE UKRAINIAN PEACE, A REPRESSED MINORITY VOICE

◆ ◆ ◆

Pacifism in Ukraine represents a minority voice, but it is an important component of the social and political landscape, especially in the context of the conflict with Russia. The peace movement in Ukraine operates in an extremely difficult context. The ongoing war has polarized society, making it difficult for pacifists to express their opinions without being accused of unpatriotism or supporting the enemy. Despite these difficulties, there are groups and individuals who continue to promote nonviolence and peace.

- Ukrainian Pacifist Movement: This group works to promote nonviolence and seek diplomatic solutions to the conflict. They organize events and campaigns to raise public awareness of the need for a negotiated peace.

- Kateryna Lanko: An activist from Kyiv committed to training in nonviolence and supporting conscientious objectors. He has been a prominent voice of Ukrainian pacifism, participating in international demonstrations and events to promote peace

The Ukrainian peace movement represents a minority but significant voice in the context of the ongoing conflict with Russia. Here is an overview of the main characteristics and challenges of the movement in 2024: The peace movement in Ukraine operates in an extremely difficult environment. The war polarized society, making it difficult for pacifists to express their opinions without being accused of unpatriotism or supporting the enemy. Despite these difficulties, there are groups and individuals who continue to promote nonviolence and peace.

Yurii Sheliazhenko, Executive Secretary of the Ukrainian Pacifist Movement, is a prominent figure in the movement. Sheliazhenko was persecuted and arrested for his pacifist activities, accused of "justifying Russian aggression" despite explicitly condemning the invasion and any kind of war. Sheliazhenko, a member of the Board of Directors of the European Bureau for Conscientious Objection (EBCO), has dedicated much of his life to promoting peace and supporting those who refuse to participate in military service for reasons of conscience.

- Promotion of Nonviolence: Sheliazhenko is engaged in educational and awareness-raising activities to promote the culture of nonviolence in Ukraine. It organizes conferences, workshops and events to spread the principles of peace and nonviolence.

- Support for Conscientious Objectors: Provides legal assistance and moral support to conscientious objectors, defending their right to refuse military service. This includes legal representation and counseling for those who face persecution because of their pacifist beliefs.

In 2023, Yurii Sheliazhenko was arrested and placed under house arrest on charges of "justifying Russian aggression" due to a statement made on behalf of the Ukrainian Pacifist Movement, despite explicitly condemning the invasion and any kind of war. His trial, set for June 11, 2024, could result in a prison sentence of up to five years. This persecution seems aimed at hindering his defense of the right to refuse to kill and his legal assistance to conscientious objectors.

International peace organizations expressed solidarity with Sheliazhenko, calling on Ukraine to drop the charges against him and respect the right to conscientious objection. Her case has attracted global attention, highlighting the difficulties faced by pacifists in conflict contexts.

Despite the persecution, Yurii Sheliazhenko continues to be an important voice for peace and nonviolence in Ukraine. His commitment and resilience inspire many, showing that the struggle for peace is possible even in the most difficult circumstances.Pacifism in Ukraine faces numerous challenges, including political repression, social polarization, and the difficulty of promoting nonviolence in a context of active war. However, the movement continues to work tirelessly for a peaceful and lasting solution to the conflict, seeking to amplify its voice through international collaborations and dialogue initiatives. The Ukrainian peace movement, therefore, represents hope for many who believe in a non-violent solution to the conflict, despite the difficulties and persecutions.

CHAPTER SEVEN.
RUSSIAN PACIFISM FROM LEO TOLSTOY TO TODAY

◆ ◆ ◆

Pacifism in Russia is a topic of great interest and complexity, reflecting the country's historical and current tensions. The roots of Russian pacifism go back to Leo Tolstoy, one of the leading exponents of Russian pacifism. Tolstoy, author of "War and Peace", played a fundamental role in the spread of pacifism in Russia. His teaching starts from the negative commandments of the Sermon on the Mount (do not kill, do not commit adultery, do not swear, do not oppose evil) and insists on the admonition "Love God and your neighbor as yourself".

Leo Tolstoy is a central figure in Russian pacifism. The fundamental principles of his pacifism include nonviolence, non-resistance to evil, non-collaboration, anti-militarism, manual labor for bread, and the rediscovery of agricultural labor. These principles are based on the Gospel teachings of Jesus, particularly the Sermon on the Mount. Tolstoy began to preach pacifism and to write more and more works, both narrative and non-fiction, on moral and religious themes. This stimulated the birth of an ethical-philosophical movement later called Tolstoism.

The matrices of Tolstoy's pacifism can be traced back to his personal existential and spiritual crisis. In 1880, while Anna Karenina was still writing, he went through a deep personal crisis that also brought him to the brink of suicide. This crisis led him to reflect on the contradictions between his ideas and his way of life. In addition, Tolstoy was strongly influenced by the thought of Rousseau and the moralists of his time. These influences helped shape his vision of pacifism and nonviolence.

Leo Tolstoy has dealt with the theme of pacifism in several of his works. Here are some of his most important books in which he talks about pacifism:

1. War and Peace: This masterpiece by Tolstoy explores the complex dynamics of war and peace through the stories of different Russian families during the Napoleonic Wars.

2. Patriotism or Peace?: In this book, Tolstoy expresses his ideas on pacifism and criticizes wartime patriotism.

3. The Kingdom of God is in You: This work is considered the culmination of Tolstoy's pacifist thought. In it, Tolstoy argues that true Christianity implies nonviolence and love for all human beings.

4. I Can't Shut Up: Against the Death Penalty: In this book, Tolstoy criticizes the death penalty and argues that violence can never be justified.

Here are some Tolstoy quotes about pacifism and nonviolence:

- *"Take the blood out of your veins and pour water in its place: then there will be no more wars."*

- *"What matters in a happy marriage is not how compatible you are, but how well you are able to handle incompatibilities."*

- *"Tutti pensano a cambiare il mondo, ma nessuno pensa a cambiare se stesso."*

- *"The two most powerful warriors are patience and time."*

- *"Do not do evil, and evil will not exist."*

- *"The Bible teaches us that having nothing to do, idleness, was the condition of bliss of the first man before his fall."*

- *"The most powerful weapon of ignorance: the dissemination of printed material."*

- *"The most powerful weapon of ignorance: the dissemination of printed material."*

These quotes reflect Tolstoy's deep belief in the power of nonviolence and love. Fyodor Dostoevsky, one of the greatest writers of Russian literature, addressed the theme of evil in many of his works, exploring the depths of human nature. However, his approach to pacifism is very different from Tolstoy's.

Another very important Russian author, Dostoevsky, cannot be considered a pacifist in the traditional sense of the term. However, Dostoevsky recognized the need for repentance and redemption. For him, even the most hardened criminal always recognizes his guilt and therefore his need for forgiveness. This could be seen as a form of inner pacifism, a search for peace with oneself and with God. While Dostoevsky addresses themes of conflict, evil, repentance, and redemption in his works, his approach to pacifism is complex and nuanced, reflecting his profound reflections on human nature and the existential condition.

Today, pacifism in Russia today is a sensitive topic, especially considering the current political context. There have been demonstrations against the current government, and many Russian artists and intellectuals have expressed their opposition to the war. There have been numerous demonstrations against the current government in Russia. Protests took place in over 50 cities in Russia. According to the independent website OVD-Info, more than 1700 people have been arrested. These protests were the most significant since the return of opponent Aleksei Navalny.

In addition, many Russian artists and intellectuals have expressed their opposition to the war. For example,

Face and Oxxxymiron, two well-known Russian rappers, went into exile for their opposition to the war in Ukraine. The arty-rock duo IC3PEAK also chose to leave the Russia before the release of their latest album. Nikita Sass is one of the few who continues to post critical videos on TikTok.

Who are Face, Oxxxymiron, IC3PEAK and Nikita Sass? They are all Russian artists known for their music and political positions:

1. Face (real name Ivan Timofeyevich Dryomin) is a Russian rapper who debuted in 2015 with his EP "Cursed Stamp". Face is known for his provocative songs and criticism of the Russian government.

2. Oxxxymiron (real name Miron Yanovich Fyodorov) is another very influential Russian rapper. He started producing music in 2008 and his albums "Posledny zvonok" and "Gorgorod" are considered among the most important releases of Russian rap.

3. IC3PEAK is a Russian musical duo consisting of Anastasia "Nastya" Kreslina and Nikolai "Kolya" Kostylev. They are known for their electronic music and their songs denouncing social problems in Russia. Like Face and Oxxxymiron, IC3PEAK has also suffered censorship from the Russian government.

4. Nikita Sass is an influencer on TikTok known for his satirical and provocative videos.

These artists represent an important voice in the Russian music scene and are known for their opposition to the war and the current government. Despite the importance of pacifism, it is often viewed with skepticism in Russia. Some argue that sending weapons to Ukraine, for example, would only prolong the agony, given the enormous disproportion of forces. Others believe that peace is one of the most important values, but recognize that the conditions of the conflict and the balance of forces on the ground and internationally influence the opening of negotiations.

Pacifism is often viewed with skepticism as in many other countries. This can be due to a number of factors, including the complexity of international conflicts, power dynamics, and the practical challenges of promoting peace in conflict situations. Some argue that sending weapons to Ukraine, for example, could only prolong the conflict, given the huge disproportion of forces. This view reflects concern that external military intervention may exacerbate violence rather than resolve it.

On the other hand, there are those who believe that peace is one of the most important values. However, they recognize that the conditions of the conflict and the balance of forces on the ground and internationally can influence the opening of peace negotiations. This view emphasizes the importance of dialogue and diplomacy in resolving conflicts, while acknowledging practical challenges.

CHAPTER EIGHT. THE STRENGTH OF ISRAELI PACIFISM

◆ ◆ ◆

Israeli pacifism has a long history of activism and nonviolent resistance, which continues to evolve to the present day. The Israeli peace movement has deep roots dating back to the 1970s and 1980s, with the rise of groups such as Peace Now (Shalom Akhshav), founded in 1978 in response to settlements in the occupied territories. This period saw growing opposition to employment policy and a push towards a two-state solution.

Peace Now (Hebrew: שלום עכשיו - Shalom Akhshav) is one of the longest-running and most influential peace movements in Israel. Founded in 1978, its main objective is to promote a peaceful solution to the Israeli-Palestinian conflict through the formula "peace in exchange for territories". Peace Now was born in response to the increasing expansion of Israeli settlements in the occupied territories. The movement aims to influence Israeli public opinion and convince the government of the need for a just and lasting peace with the Palestinian people and the surrounding Arab world.

Over the years, Peace Now has conducted numerous

campaigns and initiatives to promote peace. Among its main activities are:

- Settlement monitoring: Peace Now tracks and denounces the expansion of Israeli settlements in the occupied territories, publishing detailed reports and pressuring the government to stop these activities.

- Legal action: The movement files legal petitions to stop the expansion of settlements that violate Israeli law. - Rallies and protests: Organize marches, rallies, and other forms of protest to raise awareness and put pressure on the government.

In 2024, Peace Now continues to operate in a complex political environment. The Israeli government has stepped up de facto annexation policies in the West Bank, transferring settlement management from the hands of the army to civilian officials, a move that Peace Now considers a violation of international law. Despite these challenges, the movement remains a crucial voice for peace and justice in Israel. Peace Now is internationally recognized for its thorough and detailed work in monitoring settlements and its ongoing commitment to promoting peace. The movement continues to be a beacon of hope for many who believe in a peaceful solution to the Israeli-Palestinian conflict.

The 1990s were marked by the Oslo Accords, which brought hope for lasting peace. During this time, the peace movement gained momentum, with numerous demonstrations and initiatives aimed at supporting the peace process. The Oslo Accords, signed in 1993, represent one of the most significant attempts to resolve the Israeli-Palestinian conflict. Here is a detailed overview:

The Oslo Accords were the result of secret negotiations between Israeli and Palestinian representatives, facilitated by Norway. These talks led to the signing of the Declaration of Principles on September 13, 1993, at the White House, in the presence of United States President Bill Clinton, Israeli Prime Minister Yitzhak Rabin, and PLO leader Yasser Arafat.

The agreements aimed to establish a framework for conflict resolution through:

- Mutual recognition: Israel recognized the PLO as the legitimate representative of the Palestinian people, while the PLO recognized Israel's right to exist in peace and security.

- The establishment of the Palestinian National Authority (PA): This new entity would govern parts of the West Bank and Gaza Strip for a five-year transitional period, during which the final agreements would be negotiated.

- The withdrawal of Israeli forces: Israel has pledged to withdraw its military forces from parts of the West Bank and Gaza Strip.

In 1995, the Oslo II Accords expanded Palestinian autonomy, dividing the West Bank into three areas with varying levels of Israeli and Palestinian control. Despite initial hopes, the Oslo Accords did not lead to a lasting peace. Key issues, such as the final borders, the status of Jerusalem, Palestinian refugees and Israeli settlements, remained unresolved. In addition, violence and mutual distrust have hindered progress towards a final solution.

In 2024, the Oslo Accords are often seen as a missed opportunity. However, they remain an important point of reference in attempts to resolve the Israeli-Palestinian conflict. Discussions on how to revitalize the peace process continue, with various international actors trying to broker new arrangements. With the turn of the millennium, the peace movement faced new challenges, including the Second Intifada and the wars in Lebanon and Gaza. Despite the difficulties, groups such as Fighters for Peace (born in 2005) have continued to promote non-violence and cooperation between Israelis and Palestinians.

Combatants for Peace is a unique peace movement, founded in 2005 by former Israeli and Palestinian fighters who decided to abandon violence and work together for peace. Here is an overview of the movement:

The movement was born during the Second Intifada, a period of intense violence between Israelis and Palestinians. The founders, including Chen Alon and Suleiman Khatib, experienced firsthand the devastation of the conflict and chose to join together to promote nonviolence and reconciliation.

Chen Alon and Suleiman Khatib are the co-founders of the peace movement Combatants for Peace, an organization that brings together former Israeli and

Palestinian fighters who have chosen to abandon violence and work together for peace. Chen Alon is an Israeli theater director and activist. His personal experience as an Israeli army officer and as an artist has led him to reflect deeply on the Israeli-Palestinian conflict. After experiencing the contradiction between his role as a military commander and his artistic commitment to social change, he decided to devote himself to the promotion of peace and nonviolence. Alon was nominated for the Nobel Peace Prize in 2017 and 2018 along with Suleiman Khatib.

Suleiman Khatib is a Palestinian activist who spent many years in prison during his youth for activities related to armed resistance. During her detention, she began to reflect on nonviolence and the possibility of peaceful coexistence. After his release, he co-founded Fighters for Peace with the aim of promoting dialogue and mutual understanding between Israelis and Palestinians. Khatib was also nominated for the Nobel Peace Prize in 2017 and 2018. Together, Alon and Khatib have worked tirelessly to build bridges between the two communities through educational activities, demonstrations and dialogue projects. Their commitment has inspired many and shown that cooperation and nonviolence can be powerful tools for change.

Fighters for Peace aims to:

- End the occupation: Work to end Israel's occupation of the Palestinian territories and promote a peaceful solution to the conflict.

- Promote nonviolence: Through educational and awareness-raising activities, they seek to spread the culture of nonviolence among Israelis and Palestinians.

- Building bridges: They organize meetings and dialogues between the two communities to foster mutual understanding and cooperation.

The movement is involved in several activities, including:

- Public events and demonstrations: They organize marches, rallies, and other forms of peaceful protest to raise awareness.

- Educational projects: They offer educational programs in schools and communities to promote nonviolence and peace.

- Holocaust Remembrance Day Ceremonies: Every year, they hold a joint ceremony to commemorate the victims of both sides of the conflict, an event that has gained international attention.

In 2024, Fighters for Peace received the Organizational War Abolition Award from World BEYOND War, recognizing their commitment to ending the occupation and promoting peace.

Despite numerous challenges, including geopolitical tensions and internal criticism, the movement continues to work tirelessly for lasting peace. Their ability to unite former enemies in a common cause represents hope for the future of the region. In recent years, the peace movement has seen the emergence of new organizations and initiatives. Women Wage Peace, founded in 2014, has become one of the most influential groups, organizing marches and campaigns to promote a peaceful solution to the conflict.

Women Wage Peace (WWP) is the largest grassroots peace movement in Israel, founded in 2014 after the Gaza war (Operation Protective Edge). The movement has grown rapidly and now has over 50,000 members, with the aim of promoting a political agreement that involves women in the peace process.

WWP aims to:

- Promote peace: Work to reach a political agreement that ends the Israeli-Palestinian conflict.

- Involving women: They believe that women have a more holistic view of security, which includes not only political sovereignty and military strength, but also economic security, education, and personal security.

- Building bridges: They unite women from different communities, including Jewish, Arab, Druze, and Bedouin, to build trust and cooperation across divisions.

WWP is involved in numerous activities, including:

- Marches and demonstrations: They organize

marches for peace, such as the "March of Hope", which was attended by thousands of Israeli and Palestinian women.

- Educational projects: They offer educational programs to promote peace and nonviolence.
- International collaborations: They work with international organizations to raise awareness of the global public opinion on the need for a peaceful solution to the conflict.

In 2024, Women Wage Peace and its Palestinian sister organization, Women of the Sun, were nominated for the Nobel Peace Prize, recognizing the impact of their collective efforts toward peace and reconciliation. In addition, representatives of the movement were included in Time Magazine's "Women of the Year" list for their significant contributions to peacebuilding.

Despite many challenges, including geopolitical tensions and internal polarization, Women Wage Peace continues to work tirelessly for lasting peace. Their ability to unite women from different communities in a common cause represents hope for the future of the region.

In 2024, Israeli pacifism continues to be an important voice for peace and justice. Recent tensions and conflicts, such as those with Hamas, have led to large demonstrations and protests against government policies. Events such as the "Week of Resistance" in Tel Aviv were attended by tens of thousands of people, showing that the desire for peace and a non-violent solution is still strong.

CHAPTER NINE.
IRANIAN PACIFISM

◆ ◆ ◆

Pacifism in Iran is a complex and nuanced topic, influenced by a number of historical, cultural, and political factors. Iran has a long and complex history of internal and external conflicts, and the issue of pacifism in the country is closely linked to these dynamics. For example, there have been numerous protests and opposition movements inside Iran, many of which have expressed pacifist ideals. In Iran, there have been numerous movements and protests that have expressed pacifist ideals. However, these movements often face repression by the government. Here are some examples:

1. Woman Life Freedom Movement: This movement has seen many of its activists sentenced to death for their protests. Despite the repression, they continue to fight for human rights in Iran.

2. Narges Mohammadi: Narges is an Iranian activist who won the Nobel Peace Prize. Despite being arrested numerous times, she continues to fight for human rights

in Iran.

3. Enlightened Students: This is a group founded by Narges Mohammadi when she was a student at the university. The group supported the election campaign of reformist Mohammad Khatami.

The "Woman Life Freedom Movement" is a movement that has its roots in the Kurdish context, but which has also found resonance in Iran. This slogan has been used by Kurdish independence movements and democratic confederalism. It became a cry of call during the protests following the death of Mahsa Amini. This movement is led by women and challenges traditional, religious, discriminatory, and authoritarian norms. Despite the repression, women continue to fight for human rights in Iran. The slogan "Woman, Life, Freedom" was shouted in the streets of Iran, in classrooms, in workplaces. Women and men demonstrated side by side to claim their rights.
The response of the authorities has been ferocious: we have collected evidence of hundreds of unlawful killings, tens of thousands of arbitrary arrests, torture, rape of female detainees, intimidation of the families of victims of repression. Seven protesters were hanged at the end of irregular trials. Despite the risks, protests continue in Iran and there is great support for the population all over the world. Narges Mohammadi is an Iranian activist, vice-president of the Center of Human Rights Defenders. She is known for her fight for human rights in Iran, particularly her opposition to the death penalty. Mohammadi has been imprisoned by the

Iranian authorities since May 2016.

On October 6, 2023, she was awarded the Nobel Peace Prize "for her fight against the oppression of women in Iran and for promoting human rights and freedoms for all." Over the years, Mohammadi has been subjected to arbitrary detention, torture and ill-treatment on several occasions. Despite her serious heart and lung conditions, she was denied or delayed adequate health care.

Narges Mohammadi is one of Iran's most prominent voices of dissent and continues to fight for human rights despite difficult conditions. His story is an example of courage and determination in the fight for justice and freedom. Narges Mohammadi, during his university period in which he was studying Physics at Imam Khomeini International University, founded the group of "Enlightened Students". This group supported the election campaign of reformist Mohammad Khatami, who was elected president of Iran in 1997 and 2001.

Mohammad Khatami is known for his reformist policies and his efforts to promote civil society, democracy, and Iran's greater openness to the outside world. However, his attempts to change the system from within failed. Despite the challenges, Narges Mohammadi and the "Enlightened Students" group continued to fight for human rights and democracy in Iran.

However, pacifism in Iran is often viewed with skepticism. Some argue that pacifism can be seen as a form of complicity with the aggressor, especially in conflict contexts. This view reflects the concern that nonviolence can be interpreted as weakness or as a renunciation of resistance. Moreover, the issue of pacifism in Iran is complicated by the country's role in the region and in the world. Iran is involved in a number of regional conflicts, and its foreign policy is often seen as aggressive.

The current president of Iran is Massoud Pezeshkian, who was elected in July 2024. Pezeshkian, of Azerbaijani origin and a doctor by profession, has a long political career behind him and served as health minister under reformist former President Mohammad Khatami. Pezeshkian is known for his reformist ideas, while remaining faithful to the fundamental principles of the Iranian regime. She criticized the government on the issue of the compulsory hijab, but never called for the repeal of the compulsory veil for women. He is a supporter of the Iran nuclear program deal (JCPOA) and has vowed to improve relations with the United States, accusing his conservative rivals of ruining the economy.

However, while condemning the administration of late President Ebrahim Raisi, he never went so far as to openly criticize the Supreme Leader, Ali Khamenei. He also upheld the regime's core tenets, which say that the United States is the root cause of tensions in the region.

Although a reformist, Pezeshkian does not seem to have a direct relationship with pacifism in the traditional sense of the term. However, his political positions reflect a desire for reform and improvement of Iran's international relations. Pacifism in Iran is a complex and multifaceted issue, reflecting the country's historical and current tensions.

CHAPTER TEN. PACIFISM

IN CHINA AND TAIWAN

◆ ◆ ◆

Pacifism in China and Taiwan is a complex and nuanced topic, influenced by a range of historical, cultural, and political factors. In China, the concept of pacifism is closely linked to its history and culture. Chinese culture, which is one of the oldest in the world, dating back thousands of years, has profoundly influenced the concept of pacifism in the country. Traditional Chinese philosophy, which includes Confucianism, Taoism, and Buddhism, emphasized harmony, balance, and peace. Confucianism, in particular, promoted the idea of a harmonious society based on mutual respect and justice. However, China's history has also been marked by periods of conflict and revolution. For example, the Cultural Revolution, which took place in the second half of the 1960s, was a time of great turmoil and violence.

Despite these challenges, the ideal of peace and harmony remains an important element of Chinese culture. Many Chinese continue to support the importance of peace in international relations and society at large. However, pacifism in China today is a sensitive topic, especially considering the current political context. China is involved in a number of regional conflicts, and its foreign policy is often seen as aggressive. Despite this, in China, there are many voices opposing the war and trying to promote peace. These voices come from various sectors of society, including academics, human rights activists, artists, and ordinary citizens. Here are some examples:

1. Academics: Many Chinese academics have expressed pacifist ideals in their research and teachings. However, due to censorship and restrictions on freedom of expression in China, many of these academics prefer to remain anonymous.

2. Human rights activists: There are many human rights activists in China who have expressed pacifist ideals. For example, Li Qiaochu is a feminist, labor rights activist, and women's rights activist. Despite the arbitrary arrests, violence and torture he has suffered over the years, he has always continued his work to build a more just country that is attentive to people's rights. Another example is Xu Zhiyong, a prominent Chinese human rights activist, who was sentenced to 14 years in prison for subversion.

3. Artists: Many Chinese artists have expressed pacifist ideals in their works. For example, Cai Guo-Qiang is a Chinese artist known for his works that use gunpowder

to create explosive images. His works often express a desire for peace and harmony.

These individuals and groups often use online platforms and social media such as WeChat and Sina Weibo to express their opinions and organize peace initiatives. However, due to censorship and restrictions on freedom of expression in China, many of these efforts are hampered.

But here is to consider that for the Chinese state, these positions are subversive positions and promoters of instability and disorder. Far from peace and harmony. Every pacifist position in these countries is relative to the basic idea they have of peace: absolute order or peace to exist as a free individual. Taiwan, on the other hand, is in a unique position. The island is de facto independent and democratically governed, but China claims it as part of its territory. This situation has led to tensions between Taiwan and China, and the threat of a Chinese invasion is a constant concern for Taiwan.

Despite these challenges, Taiwan has demonstrated a commitment to regional peace and stability. However, the threat of a Chinese invasion has led Taiwan to strengthen its defense capabilities and seek international support especially with American Democrats. Nancy Pelosi, the speaker of the United States House of Representatives, visited Taiwan, officially known as the Republic of China (ROC), on August 2, 2022. A delegation of five Democratic Party lawmakers accompanied Pelosi on a visit. The two-day trip to Taiwan was part of a tour of Asia that also included stops in Singapore, Malaysia, South Korea, and Japan.US President Joe Biden discouraged, but did not prevent Pelosi from traveling to Taiwan, and the White House then affirmed her right to visit the island. Shortly after her arrival, Pelosi said her visit was a sign of the United States' "firm commitment to supporting Taiwan's vibrant democracy." The visit was condemned by the People's Republic of China (PRC), which sent warnings through diplomatic channels to the United States government. After Pelosi's departure, the PRC began military exercises around Taiwan, which took place from August 4 to 7, 2022. In this case, Nency Pelosi turned out to be a destabilizing external intervention in the area. An intervention with which Biden, at that far-sighted juncture, did not agree. In conclusion, pacifism in China and Taiwan is a complex and multifaceted issue, reflecting the historical and current tensions in both countries.

CHAPTER ELEVEN.
WAR ECONOMY.
TO THOSE WHO ARE NOT ECONOMICALLY INTERESTED IN PEACE AND TO THOSE WHO (PERHAPS) ARE INTERESTED

◆ ◆ ◆

The peace economy focuses on promoting economic conditions that foster peace and conflict resolution. However, there are powerful economic interests that benefit from war and instability. The arms industries are among the main players who have no interest in peace. These companies thrive in times of conflict, as the demand for weapons and military equipment increases significantly. According to SIPRI, in 2020 the world's top 100 arms companies had a total turnover of 531 billion dollars. As long as there is massive production of weapons, there will be economic incentives to maintain or create conflicts.

The war industries invest huge sums of money in lobbying to influence political decisions in their favor. In the United States, for example, the arms industries have spent $285 million on campaign contributions and $2.5 billion on lobbying over the past 20 years. This power of political influence makes it difficult for governments to adopt policies that promote peace. Arms industries, like other large corporations, often fund election campaigns in the United States through donations to candidates and political action committees (PACs). Some of the top defense companies contributing to election campaigns include:

1. Lockheed Martin

2. Boeing

3. Northrop Grumman

4. Raytheon Technologies

5. General Dynamics

These companies tend to fund both Republican and Democratic candidates, trying to maintain good relations with both parties. Currently, the United States Congress has approved a significant increase in military spending for fiscal year 2023, bringing it to $858 billion. This increase was supported by a bipartisan majority in both the House and Senate. The main priorities include strategic competition with China and Russia, the development of advanced technologies such as hypersonic weapons and artificial intelligence, and the improvement of the living conditions of the military and their families.

In recent times, large tech companies have significantly increased their investments in artificial intelligence (AI), and a portion of these investments are going to the arms industry. For example, companies such as Palantir Technologies are developing advanced technologies for data analysis and automation, which are also used in the military. In addition, collaborations between big tech and defense companies, such as the one between Shield AI and Boeing, are leading to the development of "digital pilot" systems for drones and combat aircraft.

The recent collapse of the world's stock markets has been influenced by several factors, including "panic selling" and global economic concerns. Big tech's investments in AI technologies, including military ones, have contributed to a climate of uncertainty. But it is also true that financial markets can benefit from geopolitical instability. In short, the arms business creates geopolitical and financial instability to create interesting opportunities for speculation. Speculation on commodities such as oil and precious metals can lead to significant profits in times of crisis. In addition, geopolitical uncertainty can increase market volatility, creating opportunities for speculators.

Geopolitical uncertainty can have a significant impact on the volatility of financial markets. When there are geopolitical tensions, such as conflicts, trade wars, or political instability, investors tend to react emotionally, often selling their assets quickly to reduce risk. This behavior can lead to large swings in stock, currency, and commodity prices.

For speculators, these swings represent opportunities for profit. Here's how:

1. Arbitrage: Speculators can take advantage of price differences between different markets or financial instruments.

2. Short-term trading: Volatility creates opportunities for day trading and other short-term trading strategies.

3. Options and derivatives: Derivative instruments, such as options and futures, allow speculators to bet on price movements without actually owning the underlying asset.

4. Hedging: Some speculators use hedging strategies to hedge against losses in other investments, while still taking advantage of market fluctuations.

Currently, several big tech and arms companies are suspected of using hedging strategies to hedge against market fluctuations. Among big tech, companies such as Apple, Microsoft, Alphabet (Google), and Amazon are known to adopt these strategies to mitigate financial risks. In the arms industry, companies such as

Lockheed Martin, Raytheon Technologies, and Northrop Grumman are among the top that use hedging to protect their investments in global operations. There is a strong correlation between the increase in war conflicts, massive investments in artificial intelligence (AI), market instability, and hedging strategies, which can be seen as part of an overall speculative strategy.

These are the points of this speculative strategy:

1. Increased war conflicts: Geopolitical tensions and conflicts can create uncertainty in the markets, leading to volatility and speculative opportunities.

2. Investments in AI: Large technology and weapons companies invest heavily in AI to develop new military technologies, which can influence market dynamics and create new profit opportunities.

3. Market instability: Economic and geopolitical uncertainty can lead to fluctuations in stock, currency, and commodity prices, which speculators can take advantage of.

4. Hedging: Companies use hedging strategies to protect themselves from losses, but these same strategies can also be used to speculate on market movements.

These elements together can create an environment in which speculative strategies thrive, taking advantage of market fluctuations caused by geopolitical and technological factors. Many conflicts are fueled by competition for natural resources. Companies that extract resources such as oil, gas, and minerals can benefit from instability, as they can obtain more favorable concessions or take advantage of the lack of regulation in conflict zones.

Companies that extract resources such as oil, gas, and minerals can take advantage of geopolitical instability and conflict zones, either by obtaining more favorable concessions or by exploiting a lack of regulation. Some of the major companies involved in these dynamics include:

1. ExxonMobil: One of the largest oil companies in the world, with operations in several unstable regions.

2. Chevron: Present in many geopolitically sensitive areas, often benefiting from concessions in conflict zones.

3. Glencore: A giant in the commodities industry, involved in the extraction of minerals in high-risk regions.

4. BP: With operations in several unstable areas, BP can obtain advantageous concessions in times of conflict.

5. TotalEnergies: Active in many regions of the world,

including countries with political instability.

Companies in the energy and natural resources sectors often fund election campaigns in the United States and other countries. Here are some examples:

1. ExxonMobil and Chevron: These companies are known to fund election campaigns in the United States, supporting both Democrats and Republicans.

2. BP and TotalEnergies: These companies also fund election campaigns in the United States and Europe, often supporting candidates who promote policies favorable to the energy industry.

The exact funding figures may vary from year to year and depend on the specific election and political circumstances. For example, during presidential and congressional elections in the United States, these companies can donate millions of dollars through political action committees (PACs) and other forms of contributions. Harris is the candidate who is most interested in high-tech funding on the use of AI in next-generation weapons and by financiers who are most interested in geopolitical instabilities in Europe. And here's why: Kamala Harris has received financial support from several prominent entrepreneurs and companies. Among big tech and companies in the war sector, Reid

Hoffman, co-founder of LinkedIn, is a major supporter.

Reid Hoffman, co-founder of LinkedIn and partner at Greylock, has had some ties to the defense industry. He is a member of the United States Department of Defense's Defense Innovation Board, a group of experts that advises the Pentagon on how to integrate advanced technologies and innovative practices into the defense sector. George Soros and his son Alex are also among Harris' funders. George Soros is a complex figure with multiple interests and activities that span various sectors. Here is an overview of its ties to the themes you mentioned:

- Immigration: Soros is known for his support of migrants and refugees through his foundation, Open Society Foundations. It has invested $500 million in initiatives that support migrants and host communities. This commitment has sparked criticism and conspiracy theories, especially in Europe, where some accuse him of wanting to destabilize the continent through mass immigration.

- Geopolitical instability: Soros has been involved in various geopolitical events, often through support for democratic movements and human rights. He has been accused of fomenting instability in some post-Soviet countries (including Ukraine) through the financing of color revolutions.

George Soros has played a significant role in investing

in Ukraine through his foundation, Open Society Foundations. Here are some key takeaways:

1. Support for civil society: The Open Society Foundations has supported Ukraine with about $230 million in donations since 1991.

2. Response to the Russian invasion: After the Russian invasion in 2022, the foundation launched the Ukraine Democracy Fund with an initial commitment of $25 million, hoping to raise $100 million.

3. Direct investment: Soros has also expressed his willingness to personally invest $1 billion in Ukraine, provided that Western countries support private investment in the country.

Donald Trump for his part received funding for his election campaign from several sources. Among the main financiers, the name of Elon Musk, CEO of Tesla, stands out, who has decided to donate the sum of $45 million a month to Donald Trump's campaign. Other notable supporters include Peter Thiel, co-founder of PayPal, Stephen Schwarzman of Blackstone, and Bill Ackman of Pershing Square. The latter are financial and investment companies. Elon Musk has shown significant interest in Donald Trump's victory. According to several sources, there are various reasons why Musk could support Trump:

1. Political influence: Musk may be interested in exerting more influence over government policy and decisions. In addition, there are rumors that Musk could get a role in the White House if Trump wins.

2. Corporate interests: Musk is engaged in several industries, including aerospace, neurotechnology, artificial intelligence, electric cars, photovoltaic panels, social networks, and superfast transportation. Support for Trump could help Musk promote his corporate interests.

3. Financial support: Musk donated a considerable sum to Trump's election campaign. This could reflect a personal or corporate interest in the outcome of the election.

4. Alliances in the tech sector: Some of Musk's colleagues and associates in the tech sector, including Antonio Gracias (former Tesla director and current SpaceX board member), investor Kenneth Howery, and Sequoia Capital partners Shaun Maguire and Doug Leone, have also supported Trump. This suggests that Musk may have shared interests with these individuals or organizations.

It is important to go and see how Sequoia has business in China.

Sequoia Capital is a venture capital firm based in Menlo Park, California, that focuses primarily on the technology industry. Founded in 1972, it has financed companies that have become icons of US high-tech such as Apple, Google, Cisco, PayPal and YouTube. Sequoia manages multiple investment funds, including specific funds in India, Israel, and China. Sequoia was recognized as the No. 1 venture capital firm in 2013. In 2014, it sold WhatsApp to Facebook for $22 billion. In 2020, Sequoia created its first European office in London, United Kingdom, and hired Luciana Lixandru to lead it. In March 2022, The Information reported that Sequoia Capital China was raising an $8 billion fund to invest in Chinese technology companies.

Back to Elon Musk. Elon is an entrepreneur known for his interests in various industries, including electric motoring, solar energy, and the aerospace industry. But there is no public information to suggest that Musk has direct interests in the arms industry.

As for relations with China, Musk has shown significant interest in maintaining good relations with the country. Tesla, for example, has struck a deal with Baidu, a Chinese tech giant, for mapping and navigation features, in order to implement its Full-Self Driving system in China. This suggests that Musk sees China as an important market for Tesla and its interests in the electric car sector. In the field of solar energy, Musk is the founder of SolarCity, a company that installs solar panels on the roofs of American homes. This indicates that Musk has a significant interest in the solar energy and photovoltaic panel sector.

Finally, as far as the aerospace industry is concerned, Musk is the founder of SpaceX, a private aerospace company that aims to make the human species multiplanetary and space increasingly accessible. SpaceX has made deals with several space agencies around the world, indicating Musk's interest in international collaboration in this area. In summary, it seems that Musk has a significant interest in pacifying relations with China, in the development of solar energy and photovoltaic panels, and in international collaboration in the aerospace industry. However, Musk's true intentions may be different or more complex.

It is important to note that these are only assumptions based on public news and reports. Musk's true intentions could be different or more complex.

Peace is not always in everyone's economic interest. Arms industries, lobbyists, financial speculators, and companies that exploit natural resources in conflict zones often have economic incentives to maintain or create instability. Or to create international partnerships, between the two poles of the world, interested in maintaining a status of order for economic purposes. However, it is difficult to establish in these circumstances where the truth lies. And the truth is always relative and linked in these cases to speculative interests. Only the poor lose in this game.

BOOKS BY THIS AUTHOR

Logistica Inversa Domestica

Find out how to turn your home into an efficient machine to save money and preserve the environment with the book "Reverse Domestic Logistics". This comprehensive guide offers a rich blend of theory and practice, providing readers with the tools they need to implement smart strategies and save money by optimizing resources such as electricity.

Through a series of practical examples and targeted advice, you will learn how to reduce energy costs in your home without compromising comfort or lifestyle. From properly organizing appliances to improving energy efficiency, this book will guide you through every step of the process, offering helpful tips and practical solutions to maximize your savings.

But that's not all: domestic reverse logistics goes beyond energy savings. You'll also learn how to reduce food waste, optimize waste management, and promote a more sustainable lifestyle.

ABOUT THE AUTHOR

Andrea Dolfi

Andrea Dolfi, born in 1983. Degree in Philosophy. Former provincial political leader. Master's Degree in Supply Chain Optimization at ELBS Business School. Master in MBA Business Administration and Management. He works as a Logistics Manager at a company that operates throughout the country. In the past he has held the role of Italy Ambassador and United Kingdom for Booking.com. 

He has already published the book Domestic Reverse Logistics, the result of professional and specialized knowledge in this new subject.

Passionate about civil rights, a convinced pacifist. He has long been interested in energy savings. Communicative Experimenter, Instagram @thetuscanianman